Following the Curve

Poems by Caryn Mirriam-Goldberg

Kansas City   Spartan Press   Missouri

Spartan Press
Kansas City, Missouri
spartanpresskc.com

Spartan Press

Copyright (c) Caryn Mirriam-Goldberg, 2017
First Edition 1 3 5 7 9 10 8 6 4 2
ISBN: 978-1-946642-23-3
LCCN: 2017950050

Design, edits and layout: Jason Ryberg
Cover painting: *Ocamora Stream*, by Rodney Troth
Author photo: Ken Lassman
All rights reserved. No part of this publication may be reproduced or transmitted in any form or by any means, electronic or mechanical, including photocopying, recording or by info retrieval system, without prior written permission from the author.

Prospero's Books and Spartan Press would like to thank Jeanette Powers, j.d.tulloch, Jason Preu, M. Scott Douglass, Shawn Pavey, Shawn Saving, Jesse Kates, Jim Holroyd, Steven H.Bridgens, Thomas Mason, Beth Dille, Mason Wolf, The West Plaza Tomato Co., Mark Mclane, the Osage Arts Community and The Robert J. Deuser Foundation For Libertarian Studies.

"What the Ocean Can Know of a Body" — Italicized words from Dar Williams' "The Ocean," used with permission.

Earlier versions of some of these poems were previously published in *Landing* by Caryn Mirriam-Goldberg, Mammoth Press, 2009, and *Chasing Weather: Tornadoes, Tempests, and Thunderous Skies in Word and Image* by Caryn Mirriam-Goldberg and Stephen Locke, Ice Cube Press, 2014

Selected Books by Caryn Mirriam-Goldberg

Poetry

*Chasing Weather: Tornadoes, Tempests,
    & Thunderous Skies in Word & Image,*
    with Stephen Locke
Landed
Animals in the House
Reading the Body
Lot's Wife

Fiction

Miriam's Well
The Divorce Girl

Memoir & Non-fiction

*Everyday Magic: A Field Guide to the Mundane and
  the Miraculous*
*Needle in the Bone: How a Holocaust Survivor & Polish
  Resistance Fighter Beat the Odds & Found Each Other*
*Poem on the Range: A Poet Laureate's Love Song
  to Kansas*
*The Sky Begins At Your Feet: A Memoir on Cancer,
  Community, and Coming Home to the Body*

Anthologies Edited

Kansas Time + Place, co-edited with Roy Beckemeyer
Teaching Transformation: Progressive Education in Action, co-edited with Lise Weil
Transformative Language Arts in Action, co-edited with Ruth Farmer
To the Stars Through Difficulties: A Kansas Renga in 150 Voices
Begin Again: 150 Kansas Poems
An Endless Skyway: Poetry from the State Poets Laureate of America, with Denise Low, Marilyn L. Taylor, and Walter Bargen

CONTENTS

Following the Curve / 1

Hold to the Center / 3

The Women Learn the Invocation to Patanjali / 4

Getting Started / 5

Healing / 6

Child's Pose *(Balasana)* / 7

Am I My Feet? / 9

Downward-Facing Dog *(Adho Mukha Svanasana)* / 10

The Yoga of Illness / 11

I Love This Body That's Not the Way I Thought / 12

Mountain *(Tadasana)* / 13

In the Middle of the Yoga Studio / 14

The Dead Poets' Yoga Class / 15

Sun Salutation *(Suyra Namaskar)* / 17

The Yoga of Memory / 18

Finding the Fire *(Tapas)* / 19

Warrior II *(Virabhadrasana II)* / 20

Body of Time / 21

Triangle *(Trikonasana)* / 22

The Yoga of Injustice, Betrayal, and Anxiety / 23

Self-Study *(Svadhyaya)* / 24

Tree *(Vrksasana)* / 25

The Yoga of Trees / 26

Balancing on the Equinox / 27

Half Moon *(Ardha Chandrasana)* / 28

What the Ocean Can Know of a Body / 29

Find Your Seat *(Uktakasana)* / 31

The Yoga of Old Wounds / 32

Devotion *(Ishvara-Pranidhara)* / 33

Prayer Twist *(Namaskar Parsvakonasana)* / 34

Let the Body Speak / 35

The Dharma of the Arms / 36

Forearm Plank *(Makara Adho Mukha Svanasana)* / 37

Pigeon *(Kapotasana)* / 38

Headstand *(Sirsasana)* / 39

Why I Do Yoga on the Tenth Anniversary
 of My Father's Death / 40

I Sing to My Bones / 41

The Yoga of Forgiveness / 42

Yoga Class Overlooking Four Oxen, Three Cars,
 Two Pick-Up Trucks, and One Blue Heron / 44

What's Pure *(Saucha)* / 45

The Yoga of Sex / 46

The Holy / 47

Corpse Pose *(Savasana)* at the End of Yoga Class / 48

Contentment *(Santosh)* / 49

Your Body is a Conversation With the World / 50

*All spiritual journeys have a destination of which
the traveler is unaware* ~ Martin Buber

To Anne and Gopi
with love and gratitude

Following the Curve

Follow the curve of your body
re-assembling itself from standing to sitting.
Your round corners unmake themselves
when you stretch out on the mat, the bed,
the old couch on the porch in the middle
of the night as the stars circle over.

Follow where the night comes from, spilling
dark ink on wet paper, changing your view.
Follow the very horizon even when it curves
into something else, another kind of body
in dappled shadows beneath telephone poles.

Follow the curve of time out of the forest
down the gravel driveway that inhales rain
and exhales daffodils to make more time.

Follow whatever curves life throws at you
as it patterns each generation and landscape
of each body curling to sleep each evening.

Listen to the arc of the tree working its edge
to catch what it can from the sun, and all else
relentlessly curving into what comes next.

Follow the river, taking what we think is fixed
into its mouth and shifting it into what wants to be
unknown again. The river of your life, your body,
aims for land, but is bent on carving new channels.

Hold to the Center

What shines here?
The sleeping coyote
in a den made of grass?
The window shade half exhaled?
The awning where ice melts?

I walk into the outside,
my long thought dissolved.
Someone or something calls,
and the hard bud on the tip
of one branch stops moving.
I don't know where the sun is
that knits all to earth's center.

I only know the way
my shoulders drop,
my jaw softens,
my eyes close
in the fresh hold
of the forgiving sky.

The Women Learn the Invocation to Patanjali

to the women in my Bhaktivana teacher training

We start *yogena cittasya padena vacam,*
the long vowels small pebbles in our mouths,
the pauses as slow water, the tremble of stone,
then the next familiar eddy to land on each syllable,
tilt it right with an inflection that lures
rain into sidewalk, hyacinth into blossom.

We want to arrive together in the lush clearing
of *sarirasya,* the hard-won leap of *yopakarottam*
to go closer to the source, the faint light
spreading slowly across the day
despite living in the age of Kali, our sore backs,
the long drought, and the small hurt telling us
we could never sing, or sing well enough
because we are never enough.

Invoke us, Patanjali, so each can sing a line of
the uncommon brail of her heart, the common book
we make together from pressed flowers from long ago,
an apple this afternoon, a long walk not yet taken.

Sing us awake, our long wings spreading,
our deep bones asking the remover
to show us our way home,
hari om.

Getting Started

seems easy as the chickadee perched
on the swing set in the storm

until the first long downward dog,
your arms searching for solace,

your breath too short on the inhale,
staccato on the out breath,

your lungs fluting memory and forecasts,
your heart amplifying the pulse,

until you bend your knees and sink to the ground
like a black colt in the moon grass.

Can you remember the lightness of no effort?
Did it ever happen, will it ever happen again

like birds landing on gutters, like rain the grass
drinks, like the easy sidewalk shadowed by iris,

a world unfolding all directions in the sunlight?

Healing

I'm a newborn giraffe, my slick legs shaking
to standing for the first time.
I'm a raw green snake that lost its skin.
I'm not a happy camper.
I'm a kitten skidding across the floor
to the rushing wall.
I'm fog that can't seem to let itself
burn into iridescence.

Do you see me in a storefront reflection?
Do you think of me when you could get up, but won't?
Do you wonder what *could* even is and how
you can be so new and broken while the world cries
in each crevice to fix it instead?

Listen to the exhausted angel, straining to reach you,
her hand on your shoulder, asking the question.
Hear the answering kestrel riding the jet stream,
no effort, all effort to surrender to the sun,
then the moon, each lifting up their reflected
and reflecting faces, then bowing
toward the dirt where everything begins.

Child's Pose *(Balasana)*

Let your toes fall on each other.
Let your forearms land, happy engines,
parked in the soft grass. Let your forehead
return to the well-trodden floor.
Let your exhalation open enough space
in the underside of your body
that a bluebird could nest there.
Let what comes breathe, tremble, stop,
look around, and close its tired eyes,
relieved to not have to be new or old anymore.

Be small, a clam wedging its way into the sand,
while your dark ponytail pours onto the mat,
the air cups your curved spine of stories
in each vertebrae of the changeable future as well
as the dusk you spent on your grandfather's lap
to watch the climbing peach roses in the alley.

Remember the sound of trees flush with wind
as he fluttered his ancient cigarette to the ground
where the birds would investigate death.
Let yourself be cradled in the cave of love.

Sweet child of mine, now, here, stop waiting.
Time is the hand you nestle in. What hurts, hurts
or stops hurting. What you think is real is nothing
compared to the breath of this body, grown or dying,
that holds this child immersed in the sweet waters
of the generous air, the lullaby of attention
carrying you out to sea, and back to shore again.

Am I My Feet?

Am I the running down a long hall of echoes
in an apartment building that holds my childhood?

Am I the grass growing through a shallow river, icy
undertow, sharp pebbles, small stories floating by?

Am I the prints left behind in the sand, or the
hungry gulls floating magnet to magnet
above the wetlands?

Am I this river I've lived, the falls and landings,
the inability to remember what happened,
then the life that could have been,
and the life that is?

Am I a water-swept upside down tree, the seeds
of the next breath, the open hand of the peony
I bend toward to smell before it's all gone?

Am I simply all this rising, climbing the sky,
then turning back to rain and river?

Downward-Facing Dog *(Adho Mukha Svanasana)*

I do not like you, downward dog.
I see right through your resting pose status
to how you're just a red-tailed hawk trying
to keep steady in the enveloping storm,
you supposed triangle, you landing base
sorting variegated fears of dying.

Turn my pelvis upside down, and bring whatever
rusting squirrels spring from the center of my body
back to the mama spine. Stop biting the undersides
of my earnest knuckles, the pads of my feet,
my forearms straining toward failure.

You think I can't tell what you're doing with me
between those graceful planks and sullen child poses?
Between the humidity of this moment,
and leaves falling outside the lines of this pose,
these walls, and the weather that keeps going
to the downward dogs?

Oh, downward dog, scatter me high and low,
breathing unsteady as winter crashing spring.
Wherever you take me, get me back to the
forgiving mat ready to exhale peonies
out of their knotty buds, and then
do it all over again.

The Yoga of Illness

Rain finally. Thunder in its tired roar.
The bare branch against the window
glistens, more precise when it's wet.
A damp chickadee waits on the same
wheel that slows my motion.
Life lays down, too tired to say much.

My head burns through the old veils
of explanation or safety.
Time to surrender like the river to the sea,
one wave of shadow or distraction after another,
a line of storms coming out of exile
to clear the street, the wind, the bench
in the distance, damp and shining.

The body quiets, goes back to sleep,
and lets the good earth breathe through it
until I wake, inhale the hum of the ceiling fan,
walk to the deck of the mourning dove,
and wait on nothing anymore but the air.

I Love This Body That's Not the Way I Thought

like I love lightning, and especially its aftermath:
a horizon balancing blue sky, dying thunderheads,
faint stars, open space—the whole world stretching
its arms two directions at once, just as I do, shaking
myself steady, remembering how this body loves
miles of sidewalk diminishing into a faint path
made by deer with genius for merging the visible.
I love the walk out of what I thought even if
my feet hurt, I'm scared by the blank stare of the sun,
or I've surrendered to how the subway sways its chant
along my spine as it cups this body in its seat.
I love the flash of yearning that turns this body
toward the dark or bright branches of sex or dreams,
all this weather informs these limbs in the seasons
that come and go, or that came and went:
the mechanisms of cell-building, the three children
from that flint-on-flint spark, the years before
walking sunsets out of housing developments,
and earlier, the fast slim legs that galloped me
down long apartment hallways as the girl
who knew how to tell herself to stay curious,
just as the woman who woke from the old pain,
and put on her walking shoes to head out into billions
of atoms shifting into fire or flower at every turn.

Mountain *(Tadasana)*

Sway if you must
as long as the legs,
inhaled umbrellas,
stand strong,
pelvis tucked,
shoulders back,
mind a tundra
few climb to the
wind-stripped pines,
child-sized, wizened
for short life, lengthening
toward light like this torso
balancing a pond
in its quiet center,
this heart bursting
into chrysanthemums,
these lungs happy as a dog
following the scent of
the next secret, these eyes,
windows open on
the first day in March,
this breath in sync with
the goose who refound
the flock sailing over
this tree, this mountain,
this woman unsteady,
smiling as the migration
makes ground once more

In the Middle of the Yoga Studio

Return to your friend, the floor, for a moment
while a plane yawns overhead, reminding you
of being a child wide awake on a bed not yours
in a building no longer standing as you wondered
who was flying above you, and where they were going.

Climb and fall into the animate and the inanimate
downward dog while at your home, right now,
a hedge apple runs furiously down the gravel drive,
and a cat sleeps on the sofa ledge.

Lean back on the bolster, your quads firing,
your scapula angling your back closer together
to show what's broken and shining in the center
of your chest to the world—all walls permeable.

Lift your chest, broaden your collarbones,
legs straight, hamstrings hugging bone,
heart both bowing and rising as the sun
pulls the tops of trees higher.

In the middle of everything, rest with all the others,
readying to lift from corpse pose while the god
of a million sunflowers turns toward the changing sky.

The Dead Poets' Yoga Class

Don't try to signal Emily Dickinson
when she's in child's pose in the back corner
she knows only as a vacant attic.
She won't see you in the space between
certain capitalized words—long dashes
designating what's beyond lines and breath.

Feel free to unroll your mat next to Whitman,
always chatty beyond expectation or good manners,
climbing his prolific butt into downward facing dog
as he yaps on behalf of all shining beings.

Frost stays at the back of the room, edging his mat away
from everyone. Don't try to make eye contact,
or he'll sigh and rattle on about the need for fences.

Shakespeare goes to the front as if he's the teacher,
blocking our view like the sun, coughing too,
abruptly and repeatedly when he should be om-ing,
and racing his eyes between clock, characters
contemplating handstands, and the long elegant neck
of the teacher, no matter the gender.

T.S. Eliot and e.e. cummings, the odd couple,
pretend they're not comparing their Warrior II poses.
Eliot rolls his eyes when cummings flips into
three cartwheels, eventually crashing into all the bolsters.
He takes a bow to wild applause.

Chaucer hates it when the teacher asks him to model
a pose, each breath a long-winded pilgrimage
to whatever fresh hell or worn-out notions of nirvana
these too-bathed humans keep inventing.

Milton doesn't show up although Byron meanders in
half-way through the class, kicks up to one headstand,
then collapses into the floor, snoring and smelling
like brandy, mud, and perfume.

The other romantics, particularly Shelley, pretend
they don't know why although Keats can't help
but burst out laughing about how yoga,
just like love, is an act of negative capability.

Sappho strolls in with H.D., rejects using a mat,
and insists on removing her gown because yoga, like life,
should be done naked. H.D. smiles enigmatically.

When it's time for *svasana,* the dead poets don't stay
in corpse pose, but chirp and crow as they lift
off their mats to roost elsewhere or fly all night,
laughing at us because we don't know how easy it is
once you release the weight of words.

Sun Salutation *(Suyra Namaskar)*

Rise up breathing. Root your stories
through the smooth stones of your soles.

Let the undertow pull down your spine,
the sea's next wave roll out your breath.

Sail strong, your chest billowing in the wind
as you return home on your own wing power.

Let the top of your head tilt forward as you
inhale into your back, and exhale out your failures.

No need to hold up all these beehives of what was
done and what wasn't. Look toward the horizon

of the windows, then fold back into the other self,
dreaming in curves and blocks of light.

Marvel at your feet before inhaling up your arms
to fly home to the ridge of the hill where you see
trees that could be horses, stones that could be birds.

Let all be beyond naming as you bow,
your palms meeting where the world holds you
all directions so you can salute the panoramic light.

The Yoga of Memory

Let the body elongate each breath and dream.
What's hurting has its own low notes.
Let the heat exhale, the chill encompass.

Let come the picture of a car parked on the shoulder,
orange berries hanging from thorny branches,
telephone wires etched in sunlight, having arrived from
the past to show the future even this is a gift,
just like the startle of the cold pond last August
when you were afraid to go further,
but the water called, and so you did.

Or that night in her father's convertible, up and down
hills in the Ozarks, topless in wind that poured thick
and variegated, Queen Anne's Lace to the right,
the yellow line ahead, as you drove into the rising moon.

Dusk filled your body then, as it does now.
Exhale. Evening swoops down outside
of how you make time.

Stand up, and walk this miracle home.

Finding the Fire *(Tapas)*
for Anne

Start with the toes, how they grip the mat,
then lift to balance the sky of your streaming words
dissolving in the fresh air.

Start with nothing but mild exhaustion,
a headache, a warehouse of excuses,
someone else's shawl falling off your shoulders.

Start with a slip of paper from an old fortune cookie
that says, *not what you expected.*

Start with whatever small will remains to try again,
knowing you will fail and fall, but welcoming the effort.

Start with wind rushing the windows. Start with
the breath, ragged because it's too hard to hold the pose,
you never could do this, and this changes the shape
of your story about a girl getting lost.

Love the art of losing things as well as the hard-won
resistance of your sore legs as you bend your knees
to sit in the middle of the air.

Whatever fire sparks in your body is enough
as the humidity of the room loosens the old skins
of what you could never do, even if you shiver
and almost fall asleep long before *svasana*.

Start with the beginning of this glimpse.

Warrior II *(Virabhadrasana II)*

Sometimes only the ragged urge to fall wins, and I forget
I'm the granddaughter of a young girl who sang her way
home through the winter woods of Poland, her voice
rough between the tunnel of black trunks.

The forgotten blue heron of my chest longs to rise
from these waters of nothing worth feeding on.
The back edge of a thunderhead surges toward me,
sucking the air out of the room. All the trembling
limbs, stupid-drunk with trying and clock-watching,
stumble to remember their roots.

The other grandmother raced fear across this continent
as she tried to make herself small enough to survive
on the crumbs of what mattered. She carried her secrets
in her pocketbook along with safety pins and stale candy.
Both women died out of their minds, broken warriors
who nevertheless would do any of it again so I could live.

The war is over, the dead long dead, as I tell the buried
grandmothers, the live grandmothers they made
out of their heartwood, the grandmother I will be
to reach our old arms wide as the canyons of loss,
strong as the occasional breeze that blesses us,
loving as all the beauty we've ever known.

Body of Time

Since the body became an I, it revels in being mine
and not yours. It bends toward drought,
and expands when it rains. It fits itself perfectly
in flannel sheets, around another body, held
in the concentric wind the ceiling fan makes.

This body of time takes another breath,
sends another valentine, ignores another blast
of unoriginal hatred as it learns new tricks:
how to hang upside down in ropes at the yoga studio,
walk across a wet field on tiptoe, or sleep standing up.

It's a month old, or 11 years, or somewhere past 57,
and while it doesn't know all the words to that tune,
it's smart enough to know how it internalizes age
like a tree does as it rings out another year.

It's all the time in the world I have,
so says the swirl of the fingerprint,
the indentation on the left ring finger,
the slight rise of a scar line on the clavicle,
the branches of veins on the back of the wrists,
the heart's muscular clutch and release.

Triangle *(Trikonasana)*

Wind, come upon me, you traveling vagabond
of rushing light across the pond, rippling calm
as I look up, over my reaching arms, spread
like a great blue heron about to lift from the water.

My face is the sun just over the cusp of trees or summer.
My torso turns up, a wheel of time catching the light.
My bloodstream is a clock of stories orbiting as dreams.
My hands, eager goldfinches or rays of long, sharp light
of the almost set sun. My eyes steady as water.
My feet planted, a good bridge across a river of stones.

Triangle, happy as any being holding the sky and ground
at once before these open windows to say, *here,*
in the expansive angles of breath, and especially
the space in between taking in the world, letting it go.

The Yoga of Injustice, Betrayal, and Anxiety

Here you are, wanting to collapse in the long-term
downward dog of all that's wrong and responsible
for the long wait, the short shrift, and the motorcycle
blast of everyone getting the hell out of here fast.

You want to rush the door, no memory of how to
trust this body so sewn to disobedience that you
collapse back into its skin of shame, and why not?
It all makes sense given what did or didn't happen.

You tell yourself this is normal, a faint crack
in the ceiling that slowly spreads while you lie,
corpse pose of course, encased in a nightmare
that whatever happened is happening again,
amplified in the dark of the dark
until a lightning bug, somehow drawn into
the bedroom of your imagination,
turns on its fire, and dissolves your thoughts.

So wake up now in the bed, in the class, on your feet,
and let yourself fall because at the very least
the earth will catch you.

Self-Study *(Svadhyaya)*

Start with the breath that knows nothing but the pulse
of the wind the lungs turns into resistance or song.

Pay attention to what's stuck or sore, gasping for air
or waking up too early in too hot a room
where the hamstrings are saying, *let it go,*
while the triceps allow you to reach just enough
toward a branch that will imagine itself into blossom.

Hold a flashlight up in the cave you've made for yourself.
If you can't see the exit, inhale the good, gorgeous dark.
Exhale open your chest to receive further instructions.

Don't ponder the clock, the others on their happy
or sad mats, or the internal weather.
Instead concentration on the real ground,
what message the windows convey in this tilt
of approaching storm, then the next wave
of change as the damp air sweeps the room,
and your tried shoulders, weary of pretending
they hold up some semblance of order.

Go back to the breath, the wind that unpacks and
scatters whatever is wanting, which is everything.

At the end, sit up, lifting your head last to be
flush with your vision. Bow to the swift cloud
swimming across the window. Study what pulses.

Tree *(Vrksasana)*

Always a lost limb—the bent leg misplaced
from gravity, or maybe dreaming it's a young
aspen tree in high summer, shining among
the dappled grass broken with Indian paintbrush
and anxious woodpeckers on their way back up.

Meanwhile, the straight leg, a long pole,
a quiet workhorse, holds up the tent of this life.
It sways in the field with the force of all its history
under the new fallen snow in the metallic blue sky.

Come inside, says the tree of the body,
from where the palms press into the mirror
of each other. *Come here,* says the spine,
balancing its river along banks that shift
with each breeze. Let the forest simply be
where all seeking refuge can return to the wild.

The Yoga of Trees

They do it all the time
because of how they must
metabolize light and wind
into motion and fruit,
whether angled down Main Street,
in Christmas light-festooned shawls,
or patterning an orchard
as the spring peepers sing on.
They've done this all their lives
from the first acorn to the last bud:
biblical yoga, age-of-Buddha yoga,
died-in-the-name-of yoga,
Mohammed and Moses yoga,
tree-loving and rock-speaking yoga,
throwing the I-Ching with their bodies,
and exhaling *Hare Krishna*
to the constellations long before
there were humans to name the sky.
All the trees meeting all the obstacles
—stone walls, volcanoes, chain-link fences,
droughts, another ice age, or traffic jam—
bent on the next twist toward light.
Before we were even seeds of ocean,
they made the roots of the world
out of their green fire,
and plowed their deaths into
mushrooms, moss, and miracles,
showing us how to practice
what makes light, what makes water.

Balancing on the Equinox

The golden tree holds her pose for seven breaths,
each one a dazzle of wind, rise, fall, feather, and run.
Behind her, a man on a bicycle lifts his hands off.
A dog tears down the street, leash flying behind him.
One white plastic bag catches on a parking meter,
spills itself to the left, and become spirit or sign
before dropping down to trash again.

I stand in the backyard in Tree: my right leg trembling
as it supports me, my left knee bent, leading back
one hip while I concentrate forward the other
to lift the spine. I press my palms together at heart center
and wish for balance even as I start to fall.
The storm to come cups the west side of this life.
The heat of summer cups the right. I exhale.
The golden tree across the way holds very still,
then surrenders everything to the wide arms of the sky.

Half Moon *(Ardha Chandrasana)*

Two directions at once without going anywhere,
yet I ache toward the horizontal, aspire to the vertical,
each breath a prayer for balance, half moon rising
in the east, half moon setting in the west.

On the horizon of the window frame, the parking garage
holds its horizontal stories of waiting and yearning,
its vertical propensity for release or homecoming.

In the space between here and there, I fall, stand back up.
The ropes hanging from the wall behind me dream
of the warm dirt of southern Mexico that birthed them
toward the softness needed for all the tension here.

The sole of my foot seals itself to the floor
while the tilted torso hungers to align itself
with something as generous as the happy roof of the sky.

Stop here, the moment says. Let whatever aches
for answers set down its many-paged agenda,
pick up its leg to reach toward where the earth ends
and begins. The light leaving. The light returning.

What the Ocean Can Know of a Body

It's known me into existance from the *wide open shore*
of nothing but starlight, and the darkness that forms all,
cell by cell in the shifting container of night
until I had no choice but to leave for the new ocean:
composed of daylight, yelling, dogs with their cold noses,
the click of light switches changing everything
I didn't yet have words for.

But the air was a false ocean—too suspectible
to weather and time, too easy for a tornado
to push around, or a drought to dissolve.
The actual ocean thinks nothing, says everything
in shiver and wave when I stand at its edge
as a small child, toeing the cold until I fall
in the foam and let the undertow take me,
my *little shoes dangling* from the folding chairs
where Grandpa chain-smoked, until I'm thrown
back into the shore of whatever fear
or miracle is next, this time, and every time
afterwards, ready or not.

I'd return as the body of a child, a woman,
some kind of mammal who remembered
what can't forget it, even if I moved to Kansas,
epicenter of all that's not ocean present, churning

shark's teeth and fossils of ocean past in its yearning
to taste the old and salty humidity of the next storm,
readying itself on any horizons I will climb over
to go 1,000 miles back or forward: arriving on
the Jersey shore at midnight, barefoot, road-weary,
trying to avoid broken glass on jagged tiers of low tide,
or into the bath waters off Florida to float under gulls
swimming the sky, or even to the bracing waters
of Maine to swim as hard as possible toward warmth,
and four singing women in the distance,
all of us aware of *how lucky we are, how precious* too
because the ocean knows change and motion,
distance and speed, and what it is to be a body,
and that body knows us.

Find Your Seat *(Uktakasana)*

Sit diagonally. Lean into your heels,
the welcoming mat, the strength
in your thighs now, the strength to come.
Give yourself to this effort while taking
your hands off the controls.

The little war your heart breaks into
in its telescopic pain is just a little war.
Fill your lungs slowly. Wait even when
cigarette smoke climbs the window
and someone laughs in the alleyway.
Reach and remember:
cricket song measures your life.

If you turn your head, a fawn in the high grass:
alone, afraid, happy. Lean forward, sit back,
and follow what you know of two birds
way above you, outside on a thin branch
weighted toward the forgiving ground. Listen.

It is not your body dissolved, your senses
inversed away from the illusion of the world.
It is this earth, this room right now,
humans hurt or thrilled, tired and waking,
willing their arms up into the sky that is
your last breath, and your next one.

The Yoga of Old Wounds

Your body clings to what waters it first swam through,
no matter how inhospitable: the asana of birth
caving in your chest, and forcing you to breathe
in the foreign air that was bound to hurt you.

A slim twisted tree at the center of your spine
trained itself to grow around the stone
(best left unturned) with a genius for dividing
and growing through the metal grates.

What you suspect happened fills in the space
between breath and tissue, hollowing out
your capacity to forgive yourself,
making new contortions out of old dead ends.

In the middle of dinner, waiting for the green light
or the conversation on the sofa,
each of us is both a single limb and the united forest:
some trees fallen to soften the hard dirt,
some just starting to climb the rungs of the weather.

All our old hurts photosynthesize what we know
to what we don't know until the rain reminds us
there's only a river that loves curves and storms.

Devotion *(Ishvara-Pranidhara)*

Surrender to the sleep that takes this body
down the tracks, a slim wave zigzagged
through milo fields and Osage orange overgrowth,
but who's to say what's inside or outside anymore?

When the motion stops, climb out of the train.
The bare ground leads to a cabin full of bunk beds
with still-damp swimsuits hanging off bed frames.

Then a test you're not prepared for: multiple choice
in dead languages that don't even translate to words.

You go outside, pick up a stick, and try to make
a circle on the bare ground, but it's too dry.
Then you realize you've always been lost.

Sit cross-legged on the curb, your bare shoulders cold,
and try to remember all the Great Lakes:
Erie. Superior, Ottawa. Michigan. One more
but before you can find out, you're back on board,
your feet dangling out the open door
as the train picks up speed.

Moon spins into view between blurs of trees,
the descent into the cooling valley of night, humming,
Hallelujah to the dark. Hallelujah to the waking
that will land you into one time and place,
where you have one task always: devotion.

Prayer Twist *(Namaskar Parsvakonasana)*

Your heart ticks at the center of your mechanics,
its hummingbird wings so quick
even your shoulders tremble
as you join your hands in prayer,

then twist your torso diagonally
toward the first shaft of sunlight after the storm,
your strong legs not afraid to run their engines
in the sweet balmy air of this room of change

where each to each, each without each,
hungers to remember how to turn away
from the narrow ruts of what we wish for

toward the space and length this body knows
as its deepest prayer before returning
to find the river has, once again, moved.

Let the Body Speak

She still sings the song of shame,
a lullaby composed of knots in the wood,
flesh too large or loose, lamented choices
made in misunderstanding.

But there is new music too
as she toes the ground of goodness,
tells herself this green light of spring
is her birthright, electric
with synapses and reflexes,
quiet as the shining reach of the heart
that travels beyond her,
then homes in to the center of the chest.

The more she listens, the more she hears
the music and light of one cottonwood tree
matching its swaying with the sun, calling out
to the world: *let all who are cold
come in from the hunger.*

The Dharma of the Arms

is the upper back, the secret side
of the heart's cradle and lung's steady dreams.

The dharma of the lungs is the atmosphere
that breathes us in, lets us go.

The dharma of the air is the jetstream,
which is the dharma of the hawk,
riding the thermals until sweeping
the wind down to the cedar tree.

The dharma of the cedar is turning light
into shelter for the nest of wrens.

The dharma of light is weather,
whose job it is to turn seed to fruit,
and body to sleep. The dharma of sleep
is to let go and trust the changing ground.

The dharma of the earth is love.

Forearm Plank *(Makara Adho Mukha Svanasana)*

When I'm hovering above the earth,
suspended on the mercy of the forearms,
the toes propping up the steel of the legs,

when I'm breathing ragged for my weakness,
sure my core will collapse into the soft
grained lake of the floor,

when I'm trying so hard not to try,
my heart slamming against its cage,
blind to where the opening is,

my shoulders take refuge in breath,
my torso makes strength out of not being
strong enough, and my eyes gaze across
the open harbor of the room
to remember I'm not alone,

then I give up, and give up again:
the heat of the moment just some heat
until it's over, and time turns
into a herd of happy antelope,
a gaggle of children pouring in the front door,
a single monarch butterfly, opening, closing
as it rests on my palm.

Pigeon *(Kapotasana)*

Twisted bird, eyes turned down
on the sad concrete of sidewalks
no one notices anymore.
One leg long extends into the future,
the other leg tucks behind
to honor all memories of flight.

I lift my chest, open the locks
of my hips to click my gaze into place.
My torso makes its usual sharp turn
toward a parking garage-framed sun
littered with trash and time.

Forgetful, I lean on my forearms,
then remember I am not
a lost bird on the ledge,
but the iridescent heart of blue,
of green, of gray seen only
when the sky slants light
across the street of wet pavement.

Headstand *(Sirsasana)*

The forearms make a cradle for the top of the head
so that the legs can unfold quickly, bowed branches
suddenly freed to the cusp of wall,
every bird in the torso trembling
in the high wind of its now-exposed nest.

Don't spill me out, the pelvis begs.
Love me enough, cry the horses of the shoulders.
Don't break any eggs, says the mind.

Meanwhile the space between organ and muscle
exhales advice to lengthen like big bluestem,
sway only when necessary, balance the lungs,
now inverted rain sticks, so that the breath
can pour down fear, love, a tree's whole coat of leaves.

Rest here in the lamplight of what you can't do
that you can do. No need to take prisoners.
It is enough, do you hear that?,
to hold strong and calm this length.

What you know now is pure gravity
that remembers underground rivers
with their vanished shores of old dreams.
Wait here for the shy gull to land.

Why I Do Yoga on the Tenth Anniversary of My Father's Death

This is my last fall, he said ten autumns ago
on his back deck, sitting in a lawn chair
in pants and a bathrobe, no slippers,
as he watched maple leaves collapse to the earth.

I sit on the floor a decade later, my right leg extended,
and lifting my heart, bend toward my knee.
I remember at the moment his slowing breath
simply stopped—a train moving so slightly
it was hard to know when it left—my hand
held his right knee until there was no more pulse.

Gone early in life with adequate but short warning,
he travels beyond the reach of our phone calls,
always brief because he was working like he had
no tomorrow. The silvering afternoon clouds
make vivid what is missing: my father's voice,
the dream of him changing what he wanted
to change dissolved like breath into sky.

I cross one leg over the other, knees stacked
like promises, and use all of this twist to see
what's behind me, what's still inhaling me taller.
No wings visible, and yet I can feel the flock lifting
off the bare tree behind me.

I Sing to My Bones

Half-way through my life,
I sing to this body, these branches
darkening against the brightness
of leaves, this knot hole
into time, the heartwood.

Flush with light, translucent
with shadow and electricity,
I used to be a child's limbs and hard sleep,
jack-rabbit fears, then joy twirling me
until I tumbled into sidewalks

Now scars from what I surrendered,
willingly, lovingly, to survive;
indentations from pain that stretched me
into another, then emptied me free.
I've given birth, and not just metaphorically.

My life is made of leaves woven from sun
and water's yearning for itself.
My skin is bewildered by years of criticism,
my size swaying on the front lawn
as the next season opens, and the last one closes,
leaving songlines across my prairies.

When all the leaves fall to husks of time,
the green light still pulses through me:
alive awake alive.

The Yoga of Forgiveness

Stop where you are. Climb down to the floor.
Lie on your belly, the left side of your face
weighted into the carpet, the right side open
to the slight waves stirring dust and light.
The air is free, as much as your lungs can hold
before exchanging this breath for the next.

Ask yourself, *What is forgiveness anyway?*
Someone's notion of no longer building a case?
A platitude you claim to show the world
you're no longer angry or broken?
A doorway out of the room of flying shards
of blame, or humid silences that never bring rain?

Push up on your hands and knees to cat/cow,
and lift your head and tail, stretching your center
into an arch. Exhale and pull back in, reversing
the curve to ask the question another way.

What is forgiveness with an apology, or without one?
What does it mean to put down your tattered shield
and say, *I still love you, I still hate you*
as you push up to downward dog.

Your quiet spine reveals the underside
of the fallen log as you lengthen into
someone bigger, less ruled by snapping resentments
and meek pleas to be let in from the cold.

Walk your feet toward your hands,
holding on to all the ground you can get.
Straighten your legs, and just be the odd girl
with her upside-down hair as she swings.
Wait for the moment to slowly rise,
your breath lifting your spine until
you're just a standing human.

Tell your mountain pose that to forgive
is not to know anymore while letting out
another inch of the kite, falling
so in love with the sky that you cry
for its pain and your own hard-heartedness.
It's all your limbs inhabiting themselves,
all your muscles holding up the muscle
of your heart, so you can offer up
what you don't even know you have.

Yoga Class Overlooking Four Oxen, Three Cars, Two Pick-Up Trucks, and One Blue Heron

for Gopi

The oxen that sun themselves on the driveway
have prayers for names, love messages in Hindi,
that make them gaze at the tender falling-down grass
with awe and hunger.

Upstairs, mats unfurled, the floor captures the last
slants of afternoon, the light moving its hips
with each new inversion of the clouds.

On my back, my feet dangling high on the wall,
I think of the sandy silk of the ox's coat,
what time it is, and how much my thighs hurt.
I breathe slowly to uncoil the terror in my throat
until we roll up to stand as mountains, still but not still.

Just over our shoulders, the blue heron swims
a current to the wetlands, alone in the grasp of sunset,
crossed through one window, then the other
until it vanishes into dusk. The cars and trucks below
dream of rusty companionship and speed.

Then we're lying in corpse pose, opening our hesitant
chests to the dark room, the whole body no longer
floating in our minds and this room, but landed
in the blue light we make time from,
all beings opening the stars of their eyes.

What's Pure *(Saucha)*

Not chastity cleverly played out by sorting
what's mine, what yours. Not a rule or diet,
a lingering ache of guilt and self-denial as familiar
as those teenage afternoons when everyone else
swam and giggled in the carnival world.

Not claiming to be always able or inept,
richer or poorer, given access to partners
or shunned from the table of love.
Not happily-ever-after or damned-if-you-don't.
Not anything on the fireplace mantle to prove
spiritual agility, and certainly not wisdom
snatched like fireflies to store in a jar until they die.

Instead, a pure moment: your spine aligned
with the mattress and whatever light comes,
your belly calm and afraid, breathing in time
with the deepest yearnings of the air.

In the middle of the night, even if there's no
moonlight available for rent, you can gratefully
touch his palm so lightly he dreams right through it,
both of you surrendered to *svasana,*
your little hearts and all their minuscule stories
blown clean in the clearing you were brave enough
to enter, letting all else fall away.

The Yoga of Sex

Start by waking up enough to love the small space
you make together, the bed its own kind of universe
blurring dreams, fear of death, joy of breath.

Reach your toes down, lift your chest,
twist from the waist toward the dark
and thunder sounding its voice to the south,
while one observant cat and errant bolt
of lightning leap down heavy, then disappear.

Unwrap the blankets to feel more skin
on skin, air on air encompassing two
as one. Stop hesitating.

Take into your arms and legs what is ready,
slow as winter landing in the woods,
quick as summer wheeling through you,
opening your life to all this falling,
past the the way you thought it was.

Then you're just a cardinal, the only fire left,
singing itself to sleep in the dark cedar tree.

The Holy

The holy does not play by our rules.
It bypasses designated creeks, preferring
high altitudes that make us nauseous.

It waits in the soft-eyed blossoms of dogwood.
It sails the air, mackerel-silvered by a distant sun.
It moves like a diagonally-landing flock
of red-winged blackbirds swooping back up
because of what's written in the sky.

The holy doesn't have arms or roots
we can weed around although the holy knows
how to hold, and hold on, rock the rocking chair,
jump rock ledge to leaf litter, then vanish.

Never saying, *Behold!* or *Alas!*
the holy inhabits one long note the women sing
in the small cabin that condenses our voices
into fog clearing before our very eyes.

Corpse Pose *(Savasana)* at the End of Yoga Class

Lights off, the forest is still. All the old trees
lie on their side or still stand, vine entwined.
The wind picks up a scent: blue car, midnight,
open windows up and down hills
in the pulse of travel.

Do you hear how thunder is always on the in breath,
glimpse of great blue heron on the out breath?
Do you know how our arms sing like sunlight
through the hinge of an open door?

The wind picks up, expanding my chest.
Without moving, I let myself land deeper
on the bamboo floor, the cement foundation,
the dirt and rock, the underground rivers
that holds the shadow side of my legs and spine.
The field between shoulders cradles the breath.

On the line my mind threads,
the bird that I call my heart,
finally lands, so grateful to be home,
before rising into the tumble of other birds,
and the thunder over the ridge of light.

Contentment *(Santosh)*

This could be the final surrender that is never final,
like saying goodbye repeatedly to people you love
without actually leaving.

This could be the flat top of the far hill
you climbed to find your lost strength,
or a thunderstorm you watched
from your front porch while the rain swept in
and lightning exhausted itself all directions,
sparking synapses, before going back inside.

This could be the simple blue afternoon
before the stratus clouds turn to ice pellets.

This could be you, a tree crossing horizons,
content as the hummingbird finding the flower.

This could be the tops of the trees blowing so hard
in sunlight that it's clear they've been in love
with motion their whole lives.

Your Body is a Conversation With the World

What are you waiting for? From the first air
in the first room, while a winter radiator breathed
enough warmth for you and your mother,
the world was chatting you up.

You gasped, you cried, you waved your tiny hands
for the ocean you left, and the story laughed itself silly
in each cell until it multiplied into millions more
marching to or denying the heart's measured drum.

Your body watches the moth on the other side
of the screen, drinks the water from the blue glass,
and jumps in its sleep, so much dialogue in this
continuing tender reckoning of bare foot on gravel,
whippoorwill telling the ears of nightfall.

You're always in conversation about how you're not
a separate animal but a talisman of your own place
alongside the freeway and the prairie,
each step another word, each shrug another question
for the lightning bug caught on the ceiling,
the cat leaping from refrigerator to your shoulder,
the wind or its absence evident in the still grasses.
The answers may knock you over or have nothing
to do with the question you're pacing across the day.

Time tells its stories through your body,
so yoked to this love that it cannot stop singing.

Acknowledgments

Finding yoga was one of the biggest surprises of my life. Yet in my early 40s, when I began chemotherapy for breast cancer, I started craving yoga, and I was lucky to find Karen Seibel's one-on-one yoga classes. I eventually made my way to yoga classes with MariaAna Garza, and after some years, shocked myself by declaring I wanted to become a yoga teacher. I was very fortunate to land in Gopi Sandal's first yoga teacher training with a powerful and loving group of women. Throughout the last decade, I've studied with Anne Underwood, and over many years, I've learned a lot about grace from Laura Ramberg. Bouquets of peonies to all these women for teaching me how to come home to my body and the world.

My husband Ken, and two of our children, Natalie (also a yoga teacher) and Daniel, are devoted to yoga, which sweetens my practice immensely.

Thanks also to Spartan Press and Jason Ryberg, who took on the big, tedious, and often-unsung task of helping many writers get their poetry into print. Deep appreciation to Jeffrey Ann Goudie for suggesting the title of book over lunch one day. Much gratitude to Rodney Troth for opening his visionary studio up to me, and letting me choose one of his paintings for the cover of this book.

Caryn Mirriam-Goldberg, Ph.D., the 2009-13 Kansas Poet Laureate is the author of over two dozen books, including *Miriam's Well,* a novel; *Everyday Magic;* and the award-winning *Chasing Weather: Tornadoes, Tempests, and Thunderous Skies in Word and Image* with weather chaser Stephen Locke. She curates 150KansasPoems. Wordpress.com, out of which three anthologies have been published, including the recent *Kansas Time + Place,* co-edited with Roy Beckemeyer. She's co-editor of *Konza: A Bioregional Journal on Living in Place.* Founder of Transformative Language Arts at Goddard College where she teaches, Mirriam-Goldberg leads writing workshops widely, and with singer Kelley Hunt, writing and singing retreats. Caryn completedthe Bhaktivana Yoga with Heart teaching training program with Gopi Sandal, and Anna Guest-Jelly's certification in teaching Curvy Yoga. She regularly studies with Anne Underwood at the Yoga Center of Lawrence, and with the sky, trees, and prairies in her backyard. www.CarynMirriamGoldberg.com

Rodney Troth is a long-time painter (acrylics, watercolors, and oils) who says, "The landscape has always been the primary draw—the reverence for the environment, and paying attention to the environment have always been my main source of inspiration." He credits this perspective from painting extensively with Robert Sudlow, who had a deep spiritual connection to place. A voracious reader constantly influenced by outside sources, Troth studied architecture, painting, and poetry at the University of Kansas. He's had shows of his paintings in St. Louis, Kansas City, Chicago, and New York, and his work has been widely featured in Kansas.

"Ocamora Stream," the painting he contributed to this book cover, came from working with a compelling New Mexico landscape. He says that the scene he painted has "....a different kind of light, topography, color, palette, and I just had an explosive reaction that I needed to capture as much as I could as quickly as I could." Troth explains the he paints to understand what's happening, and in the process, develops a keener sense of observation that becomes part of his artistic vocabulary.

www.ingramcontent.com/pod-product-compliance
Lightning Source LLC
Chambersburg PA
CBHW021451080526
44588CB00009B/801